Old CLACKMANNAN, SAUCHIE, TULLIBODY and other airts of the Wee County

by
Guthrie Hutton

Alloa Road, Tullibody, looking towards the junction with Menstrie Road and Stirling Road. The Abercromby Arms, the dormer-windowed building in the background, is about all that remains from when this picture was taken before the First World War.

© Guthrie Hutton 2003
First Published in the United Kingdom, 2003,
by Stenlake Publishing
Telephone/Fax 01290 551122

ISBN 1 84033 238 7

Devon Village is little more than a row of cottages adjacent to Fishcross. It was where David Halley lived, and kept his fleet of three buses which he ran between Alloa and Tillicoultry, passing through the village on the way. He is seen on the left outside his house with his mechanic and one of the buses.

Bob McCutcheon: An Appreciation

Some of the pictures in this book come from the collection of the late, and much lamented, Bob McCutcheon, formerly of the Book Shop in Stirling. The untimely death of this great character has robbed local history in the Stirling and Clackmannan areas of an enthusiast and a huge fund of knowledge. Bob helped me with projects relating to canals, mining and other topics. He has been a friend, an inspiration and an invaluable source of material.

ACKNOWLEDGEMENTS

I am indebted to the Scottish Mining Museum at Newtongrange, Midlothian, for permission to use the pictures on pages 14, 25 and 37. I would also like to thank Peter Stewart, Alan Geddes, Robert Grieves and Margaret Graham for providing pictures for this book; without their contributions it would not have been possible.

SOME FURTHER READING

The books listed below were used by the author during his research. None are available from Stenlake Publishing, and anyone interested in finding out more is advised to contact their local bookshop or library.

Clackmannan Libraries have produced a number of excellent local publications including:

Adamson, John, *Sauchie and Alloa: A People's History*, 1988
Kirk, Robert, *Historical Sketch of Tullibody Part 1*, 1983
Kirk, Robert, *Historical Sketch of Tullibody Part 2*, 1992
Lothian, James, *Alloa and its Environs*, 1861, reprinted 1983
Ure, Adrian, *Local Railways*, Volumes 1 and 2, 1986/87

Other titles referred to were:

Carvel, J.L., *One Hundred Years in Coal*, 1944
Day, J.P., *The Counties of Clackmannan and Kinross*, 1915
McMaster, Charles, *Alloa Ale: A History of the Brewing Industry in Alloa*, 1984
Murray, Ian, *From the Forth to the Devon in Old Picture Postcards*, 1996
Swan, Adam, *Clackmannan and the Ochils: An Illustrated Guide*, 1987

INTRODUCTION

A story is told of how Lookabootye Brae at Clackmannan got its name – King Robert the Bruce apparently lost a glove while hunting, and sent some men to 'look aboot' for it, finding it at the brae. Whatever the truth of this tale, Clackmannanshire adopted 'Look Aboot Ye' as its motto. I first became aware of it on the county badge on my Boy Scout shirt. Two things struck me: I could understand it – it wasn't in Latin – and it seemed like good advice which I have adhered to ever since. In many respects this book, and others like it that I have compiled, are the result of me 'looking aboot', observing and noting the everyday lives of people and places.

The 'wee county', Scotland's smallest, was originally bounded by marshlands to the west and a forest to the east, and with the Forth and the Ochils to south and north it was like an island, with access difficult on all sides. The original seat of power and influence was Clackmannan itself, but it was eclipsed as the county town by Alloa as it grew in industrial and commercial importance. The little village began to decline, sustained and bolstered for a time in the mid-twentieth century by the mining industry.

Mining is the common thread running through the story of the villages across the county. Sauchie was originally the seat of a powerful family, but the area was also rich in coal and efforts to exploit it led to big changes. One of the earliest railways in Scotland was laid to get the coal from old Sauchie to ships at Alloa harbour. On its way it passed a scatter of miners' cottages that through time expanded to form the separate community of New Sauchie. The mining industry had prospered there, while languishing in other parts of Scotland, following development of the Gartmorn dam which provided the power to drain water from the pits.

Tullibody too was shaped by coal although it can claim its origins as a settlement to an earlier time. Kenneth MacAlpine, King of the Scots, set up camp nearby in AD 834 before defeating the Picts in a battle which had the effect of uniting the two peoples into a single nation, although at the cost of a subjugated Pictish people and culture. The Scots' victory was commemorated by a carved stone cross which survived into the nineteenth century and was replicated for the Tullibody and Cambus war memorial. Tullibody was in the wars again in 1559 as Catholics and Protestants struggled for supremacy. In more modern times the village was transformed by the coal industry and then left in the lurch when the super-mine of Glenochil failed to match the grand plans the industry had for it.

Mining in the wee county continued at Castlebridge pit up to the end of the twentieth century, but Clackmannan, Sauchie, Tullibody and other nearby villages are now 'looking aboot' for new ways of keeping the story going through another century and beyond.

Linn Mill

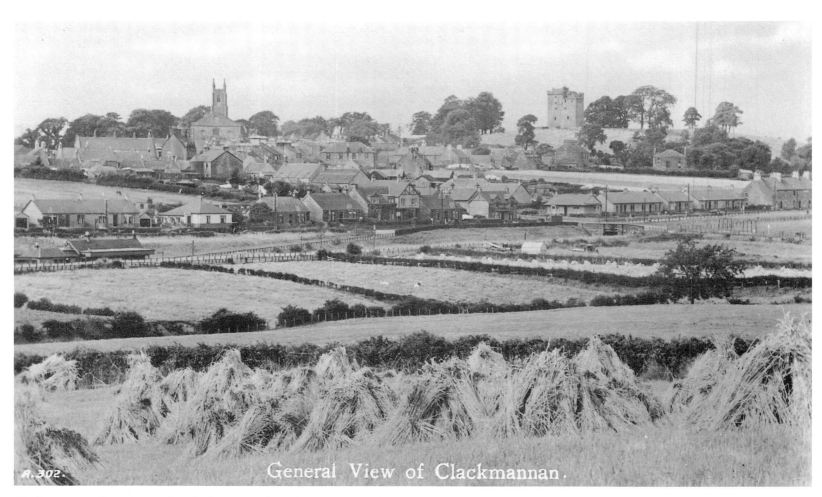

General View of Clackmannan.

Clackmannan village is seen here looking west from the minor road that used to run between Dukestreet and Tulligarth. The ground behind the stooks of corn in the foreground dips away to the Goudine Burn and beyond that the Alloa & Kincardine Branch Railway. The roof of Clackmannan and Kennet station is just visible on the left. The picture gives a good indication of the way the village is clustered at the base of King's Seat Hill, which is crowned by the twin symbols of early power, the castle and the church. There has been a church here since the thirteenth century, but the Parish Church building in the picture was erected in 1815 at a time when Clackmannan's influence as a county town was declining and shifting westward to Alloa.

King's Seat Hill is a natural defensive site commanding the Forth and the country around about. It takes its name from the early kings of Scotland who, in recognising its strategic advantages, appear to have built, and occasionally occupied, some form of structure on the summit throughout the turbulent twelfth and thirteenth centuries, and possibly before that. Anxious to offload the responsibility, King David II sold it to his kinsman Robert Bruce in 1359. Although this Robert Bruce was of royal descent he was not involved in weighty matters of state and settled for the life of local laird to the people of the little village below the great house. The first phase of Clackmannan Tower, the shorter tower on the right of this picture from the 1890s, dates from his time. The taller tower, and the battlemented tops of both date from the fifteenth century. A mansion house was erected alongside the tower in the late sixteenth century and further enhancements were made to it a hundred years later. The decorative doorway, just visible behind the stone wall in the left foreground, was added at the same time. The last of the Bruce family, Lady Catherine, died in 1791 and subsequent owners allowed the mansion and tower to fall into disrepair. Mining subsidence also threatened the stability of the structure which nonetheless still sits atop its hill, a superb example of the architecture of its time but one that is in sore need of a revival to make it more accessible and perhaps give the village a focus again.

The Ochil Hills dominate any view to the north of Clackmannanshire as this picture, apparently taken from the tower of the Parish Church, shows. If photographed today the view would reveal that new housing now occupies the foreground fields, and also some of those in the middle distance. The older terrace of houses in the centre of the picture is known as Tower View; in front is the Tower Hotel and to the right the former manse of the United Protestant Church. On the left, from behind the trees of the Back Wood, the road to Alloa heads up the brae from the Mary Bridge over the Black Devon River. To the right of the road is the cemetery, and behind that the junction of the Stirling to Dunfermline Railway and its Alloa & Kincardine Branch line, which cuts across the picture above the houses. The distinctive peak, rising from the folds of the hills in the centre background, is Ben Cleuch, the highest of the Ochil range at 2,363 feet above sea level.

Clackmannan's High Street runs down the spine of King's Seat Hill to where it forms a crossroads with the old Alloa to Kincardine road and Main Street. At the point shown here the streets widen out in the classic style of old Scots villages to form a market place, the one-time centre of village, and indeed county life. The tolbooth, where civic business and administration of the law was conducted, stands slightly to one side of the market place. It was built in the late sixteenth century and the distinctive tower added about a hundred years later, but only this and the adjacent gable wall of the original building remain. The clock was added to the tower in 1866. Of the other buildings in this picture from around 1900 most of those immediately to the right of the tolbooth have been replaced, while the one behind and to its left has also gone.

Standing adjacent to the tolbooth are two other symbols of significance to both village and county – the market cross and the Stone, or Clach, of Mannan. The cross was erected in the sixteenth century prior to the building of the tolbooth and has the Bruce family arms carved at the top. The Mannan Stone, from which the county takes its name, is somewhat older having originally sat by the shores of the Forth where it was used for pagan worship before the people were converted to Christianity. It was mounted on its stone plinth beside the cross in 1833. Main Street runs down the lower slope of the hill from the market place before narrowing and becoming the street called the Cattle Market. Just creeping into the right-hand edge of the picture is the distinctive gable of the old Royal Oak Hotel, which still survives as a building although the almost adjacent Commercial Inn has gone.

Looking back up Main Street, this picture from the mid-1920s is dominated by the library building on the left which also once contained reading and billiard rooms. The building was erected in 1903 as a gift to Clackmannan from Alloa's wool magnate John Thomson Paton. A further donation, from the foundation set up by Scots American entrepreneur Andrew Carnegie to fund public libraries in Scotland, helped to provide books. The library sat in front of the 1888 town hall building giving it a much grander entrance. Many of the other buildings in the picture have been altered or replaced, but the most obvious change is that Clackmannan Health Centre now occupies the site of the building on the right.

PUBLIC SCHOOL, CLACKMANNAN.

Clackmannan Public School occupied a site between the Alloa to Kincardine road and the railway. It was built in 1897 and could accommodate up to 400 children in eight classrooms. The school was extended a number of times over the years. The re-entrant corners of the original T-shaped building were filled in to make it into a large rectangular mass, various outbuildings were erected in a corner of the playground and single-storey wings were added to each end of the main school. As the buildings expanded, they took up more and more space leaving the children only a small tarmacked playground in which to let off steam. At least, parents permitting, they could escape to the country after lessons.

A + A. MITCHELL'S SELF BINDER.

Like the illustration on page 5, this late nineteenth century picture of a reaper/binder was intended to be viewed through a stereoscope – a device for looking at photographs that made them appear three dimensional. The exact location is unknown, but it was almost certainly taken in Clackmannanshire, being found amongst other pictures which were predominantly of the county. The A. & A. Mitchell in the caption could refer to the brothers Andrew and Alexander Mitchell who were partners in the Clackmannan Coal Company, and later the Alloa Coal Company. They owned a number of farms around Alloa and Forestmill and were noted for breeding shorthorn cattle. The reaper/binder (if the guess as to its ownership is correct) would indicate that they also grew crops.

The row of late eighteenth century cottages that make up the bulk of Kennet village is typical of the kind of housing provided for miners and their families throughout the Scottish coalfield. Miners' rows, made of either stone or brick, and sharing common gables along their length to reduce building costs, often consisted of only single rooms and had no proper sanitation. A *Glasgow Herald* reporter wrote a series of generally damning articles about such rows in 1875. In his travels he looked at some in the vicinity of Clackmannan, although not apparently at Kennet. He had expected to see a better standard of dwellings in the county than those he had encountered in Lanarkshire, but at the Pottery, Westfield and the Green he was depressed to discover much the same damp and insanitary dwellings as he had visited in Scotland's 'Black Country'. Now Kennet's row has been restored and the cottages give the appearance of being very desirable residences.

In old Scots a waterfall was known as a linn, while in Gaelic the word 'linn' refers to a pool below a waterfall; using either definition there was a linn on the Black Devon where a grain mill was established in the late seventeenth century. The linn was a natural site for a mill with water being taken from the higher level to drive the wheel lower down. The original mill was superseded by others, the last being a sawmill which had become disused by the time this picture was taken in the early twentieth century. Fishing in the pool below the waterfall appears to have been a popular sport.

Castlebridge shaft was part of the complex of mines developed to provide coal to the Longannet power station. The first mines, Bogside No. 3, Castlehill and Solsgirth were to the north of the power station and were driven into a seam of coal known as the Upper Hirst. They were linked together by a five-and-a-half mile long underground conveyor belt, one the marvels of Scottish engineering, but one that few people know about because it was below ground and out of sight. The mines started sending coal down the conveyor to Longannet in 1970, but as the workings advanced away from the access mines they reached a distance and a depth which demanded a new access. This was made in the form of a shaft, sunk just south of Forestmill, and was called Castlebridge – a name invented in a competition for local schoolchildren who combined the names of Castlehill and Kincardine Bridge. The shaft was in use from 1986 up to the end of the year 2000 when new faces were opened up under the Forth. In March 2002 these were inundated by a catastrophic flood which forced the abandonment of what was Scotland's last deep mine.

Forestmill takes its name from a former mill on the Black Devon River in the great Clackmannan Forest. The village would have grown up around the mill and farm, and, although modified, some of the buildings in this early twentieth century picture still survive. The line of the road between Kincardine and Kinross has not been greatly altered where it passes through the village, although the carriageway is now much wider and faster – and walking down the middle of it carrying a bundle of sticks would be a touch risky today. As the road passes through the village it also crosses a bridge over the Black Devon and an adjacent culvert over a man-made lade. The lade is two miles long and almost 300 years old, and was made to feed water from the river into the Gartmorn Dam. The sluice gate which originally controlled the flow has been superseded by a more modern one, but still exists close to the road.

Gartmorn Dam, Alloa.

It may seem odd to collect a huge body of water and then use it to prevent water gathering elsewhere, but that was precisely the function of Gartmorn Dam. It was a marvel of early eighteenth century engineering and was the brainchild of engineers working for the 6th Earl of Mar. Their idea was to provide a head of water to drive pumping machinery which would drain water from his coal mines. It was highly successful, but when this use of water power was eventually superseded by steam the dam's original function ceased. The great reservoir – the largest in the country when it was made – was taken over by the county for domestic water supply and is now the focal point of a country park.

The system employed by the Earl of Mar's engineers took water from the dam and fed it along a lade to drive water wheels. This one was at a pit near Sauchie. The power of a large water wheel can be awesome and here it was transmitted to the rocker arms mounted on the masonry column. These in turn were connected to pump rods fitted with buckets which lifted the water in stages from the mines. To people accustomed to the technological wizardry and sophisticated engineering of the modern age, this might seem antediluvian, but it worked. Furthermore it worked at a time when minewater elsewhere was severely retarding the development of the coal industry and posing a serious danger to those underground. Sadly, although this wheel was still working up to the mid-nineteenth century, and survived into the early twentieth when this picture was taken, nothing of it now remains, although the cottages beside it still exist.

Unlike its older neighbours, Clackmannan and Alloa, Sauchie has only been a distinct community for a comparatively short time. The original Sauchie clustered around the tower house known as Sauchie Tower (see page 27), but as mining developed to the south so did a new village. Miners' housing in the form of individual rows, or in more communal groups such as Holton Square, eventually coalesced into an identifiable village which was recognised as such and officially named New Sauchie in 1891. This picture of Main Street was taken about ten years later.

Co-Operative Society, Main Street, Sauchie.

The centre of the village was spread along the main road from Alloa to Tillicoultry with the focal point – typically for a mining village – being the co-operative store. The first co-op in the village, the Newtonschaw Co-operative Society, was formed in 1865 and the drapery, which appears to have been a major part of the society for many years, was established in 1873. The main co-op building in this view was erected in 1913.

Few buildings seen in these early views of Sauchie Main Street survived its wholesale post-war redevelopment, but the main co-op building was one, as was Graycraigs House, the large mid-nineteenth century building on the extreme right. Its name is inscribed on the band of stone running between basement and ground floors, confirming the spelling as 'gray' with an 'a' and not an 'e'. Graycraigs was apparently associated with the Devon Ironworks and presumably their successors the Alloa Coal Company, and was where miners at the local pits were paid. The building is also thought to have operated as a truck shop which, if correct, would mean that the miners received their pay in the form of tokens which had to be redeemed at the shop in exchange for overpriced provisions. The old mining companies justified the system as a way of ensuring that families were fed before the men spent money on drink, but there was no alternative, so the employers simply took away with one hand what they had just paid out with the other. It was an iniquitous system which bound people to the company in circumstances not far removed from slavery.

A pram, home-made from an old box, sits outside a house in Fairfield which leads out of Sauchie towards Alva. The field, after which the area takes its name, was literally the field where fairs were held – events where produce and stock were bought and sold, and people presented themselves for hire for agricultural work. There is still a public park in Fairfield Road, on the left beyond the old stone houses. However, there are now many more houses above and beyond those on the right. Two early miners' rows, Reekie Row and Holton Row, stood on either side of Fairfield, at its south end, and the colliery wagonway from the Devon Collieries crossed the road between them and ran for a short distance alongside the road.

Sauchie Public Hall, on the corner of Fairfield and Mar Place, is a superb building designed by the notable Alloa architect William Kerr. It was erected in 1911, extended to Kerr's designs in 1925 (as seen here), and later extended again, although this last and uninspired addition sits uncomfortably with the quality and style of Kerr's earlier structures. The original building was paid for by local subscriptions, but later extensions and ongoing maintenance were funded out of grants from the Miners' Welfare Fund. The fund was set up under the Mining Industries Act of 1920 and was the first of its kind where a charge was imposed on an industry for the welfare of its workers and their families. A penny had to be paid by the mine owners on every ton of coal mined and four fifths of the money had to be spent in the area where it was raised. A local committee made up of both owners and mine workers determined how it would be spent.

The Miners' Welfare Fund could be used for a variety of purposes and was not confined to institutes and public halls. In Ayrshire there was a preference for rehabilitation homes, in Shotts the fund built a swimming pool and in Kilsyth it paid for a large complex of sporting and recreational facilities. In Sauchie, and in Coalsnaughton, it was used to provide children's playgrounds; this is the one in Sauchie. Today's child safety legislators would probably be horrified by the hard surfaces, the roundabout which could trap little feet and the unguarded slide, but youngsters in those pre-video days would have found these facilities exciting and wonderful, and would have played happily on them for hours.

The Miners' Institute at Fishcross was built in 1930 by the Miners' Welfare Fund and, like the public hall in Sauchie, was designed by William Kerr. He contrived to make the Fishcross Institute appear like a small version of the one at Sauchie by incorporating many similar architectural features into it, such as the Dutch gable over the door and the large hall window. The village of Fishcross originally consisted of not much more than a couple of rows of miners' cottages, but more and better miners' housing, like that on the left of this picture, was built as the adjacent Devon Colliery grew. The colliery had a complex evolution. Its principal installation was known as Furnacebank Pit and supplied fuel for the Devon Ironworks which was established in 1792. The pit continued in operation up to the 1850s, but a decade later had been abandoned due to water ingress and it lay disused until the Alloa Coal Company took it over in the late 1870s.

Devon was the deepest colliery in the county, acting like a sump for the rest of the coalfield to drain into, and a number of pumping engines were needed to keep it dry enough to work in. This Cornish beam pumping engine house was erected in 1864 by Neilson of Glasgow, but was only fully equipped to operate as a pump by the Alloa Coal Company when they started to drain the flooded workings in 1879. It took a year to clear the water at a rate of eight million gallons every twenty-four hours. When the pit was drained and coal production restarted, this and other pumps remained in constant use. A generating plant was installed at Devon in the late 1930s for all the Alloa Coal Company operations in the area, and electric pumps superseded the beam engine, but it remained in reserve – just in case! It is now one of only two such engine houses in the country still *in situ*, and still with their huge cast iron beams in place (the other is at Prestongrange, East Lothian).

During the Second World War Devon's miners were known as the output champions of Great Britain and they continued as pace-setters after the war with a rate of extraction from three-foot seams of 40 hundredweight per man. The 490 men also set a Scottish record when they turned out 980 tons in a day; little wonder then, when the closure of Devon was announced in the late 1950s, that this previously hard-working workforce reacted badly. They staged a stay-down strike, a form of protest in the mining industry where men refuse to come to the surface. Of the 62 men who started the protest, 57 remained underground for 52 hours until their union leader persuaded them to come up. The effort, sadly, failed to alter the decision and the pit closed in March 1960. The colliery chimneys can be seen in the background of this early twentieth century picture looking along the Devon River to Devon House. This was built for one of the partners of the Devon Ironworks and remained associated with the colliery, and virtually surrounded by it, through various changes of ownership.

Sauchie Tower was another, more historic house that found itself surrounded by Devon colliery. The barony of Sauchie was granted by King Robert the Bruce to a Henri de Annand in 1321. One of his two co-heiresses married into the influential Schaw family and they ultimately acquired the whole property. They built Sauchie Tower around 1430/1440 and it remained the family's principal residence until 1631 when they built a mansion house alongside. The family moved again, 70 years later, into a grand mansion at Schawpark and in 1752 the estate passed by marriage to the Cathcart family. By the mid-nineteenth century the internal timbers of the old tower were described as 'fast decaying and falling down'. The building was sold in 1982 for 'an old Scots penny' in the hope that the new owner would restore it, but it remains a semi-derelict shell with a temporary roof, cables binding the walls to stabilise the masonry and bricked-up windows.

For a time Marchglen was the location of Tillicoultry's first station and the terminus of the Devon Valley Railway, but the little village lost this exalted status when the viaduct was built to carry the railway over the river and into Tilly itself. No doubt Marchglen would have sunk back into obscurity had not G. B. Johnstone taken up hand loom weaving; by advertising his wares with this postcard he made people aware of Marchglen. He began weaving in the 1880s and for many years plied his trade beside Loch Katrine, but when a local by-law stopped him from working in a public place he was forced to move his pitch in the 1930s. Undeterred, he set up on a piece of private ground at Lochearnhead and carried on weaving. He is seen here operating his rickety-looking loom, with some of his fine cloths displayed on his car which sports the old Clackmannan registration letters SL.

The large mansion house of Dollarbeg, on the ridge above the Devon to the south of Dollar, was built about 1900. Initially the family home of a tobacco magnate, it was taken over by the London-based Workers' Travel Association which opened it as a hostel-cum-hotel in July 1934. People came to it from all over the country to enjoy a holiday in the Clackmannanshire countryside. 'It is a wonderful place' wrote one happy holidaymaker, who was 'having a wonderful time', while also expressing surprise that the weather was 'actually quite good'. During the Second World War it was taken over as a Royal Air Force base and anti-aircraft battery, and continued as a hostel/hotel for a time after the war.

Although the name Coalsnaughton apparently comes from an ancient woodland, the 'coal' element of it could hardly have been more appropriate for a village sustained for many years by mining. Even the main street running through the village is named after R. B. Wardlaw-Ramsay who owned pits in the Lothians as well as Tillicoultry House and estate. This western end of the street is Wardlaw Street while the eastern end, from the junction with Main Street, opposite where the United Free Church is seen on the right, is known as Ramsay Street. The church and manse have survived, and while the street is now much changed to cope with the demands of modern traffic it retains the same line. The cottages on the left have all gone, but the one in the right foreground has survived to keep the church company into the twenty-first century.

Public Hall & Library, Coalsnaughton

"The T.W.S" Series

Coalsnaughton Public Hall and Library were built in 1907, with ornate plaques above the doors to indicate which entrance was which. A lesser hall was added in 1925 which, like Sauchie Public Hall, was designed by Alloa architect William Kerr. This picture was used as a postcard in 1919 and shows the building before the extension was added, on the left, and before the war memorial was erected on the corner of the perimeter wall and fence facing the camera.

Going out of Alloa along Tullibody Road in the early twentieth century, past the Forester-Paton family's great houses of Inglewood and The Gean, the countryside was largely unspoiled. This picture was taken from a spot somewhere near to where Thorne Road now runs alongside the main road. In the background is Dumyat, the prominent hill at the western end of the Ochils, and on the lower ridge, in the centre of the picture, is what appears to be Lornshill farmhouse. In the foreground is the Fairy Burn, a favourite spot for Alloa youngsters who used to wander out of town to fish in it for minnows.

This picture of Alloa Road, Tullibody, was used as a postcard in 1904 although it may have been taken a few years before that. At the time there was farmland and countryside between Tullibody and Alloa, but now the built-up area is almost continuous, with the fields on the right here having been taken up by housing many years ago. The muddy and rutted road surface has also been improved which would no doubt have given Jim, the cyclist in the inset picture, a more comfortable ride on his boneshaker. He was photographed in 1905 leaning against the wall of a house in Alloa Road. The churches in Menstrie Road can be seen on the right of the main picture.

ALLOA ROAD, TULLIBODY.

The east side of Menstrie Road, Tullibody, is lined by a remarkable group of church buildings. The Auld Kirk, now ruined and roofless, dates from the sixteenth century. The roof was taken off in 1559 by French troops in the service of the Queen Regent, Marie de Guise, Mary Queen of Scots' mother. The Catholic French had been in Fife, but when a Protestant English fleet cut off their route back to Edinburgh they retreated towards Stirling to cross the Forth there. They found an arch of the bridge over the Devon at Tullibody had been destroyed and so they repaired it with the roof off the church.

George Abercromby of Tullibody House had the Auld Kirk reroofed and restored about 1760, but by the early twentieth century the structure had become unsafe. It was again unroofed and abandoned in 1904 when the remarkably simple and unostentatious new St Serf's Parish Church was opened.

Alongside the Auld Kirk is the church hall building which was originally erected in 1844 as the Free Church. In 1843 a schism opened up in the Church of Scotland. The reasons are complex, but at the heart of what became known as 'the Disruption' was the right of congregations to choose their own ministers instead of having someone favoured by a strong patron being imposed on them. Most of Tullibody's churchgoers seceded from the established church along with the assistant minister Mr Stevenson. In view of their numbers they were able to build a new church, adjacent to the old, more quickly than happened elsewhere. Often these adherents to 'The Church of Scotland Free' had to meet in whatever accommodation they could find until they were able to build a new church. Tullibody's congregations had reunited by 1951 when the Free Church building became the church hall. It is on the left of this picture with the manse, which dates from 1847, in the centre.

The Tan Works, Tullibody.

Dumyat appears in the background of this view of the tannery at Tullibody, seen from Alloa Road with New Row, or as it was later called Delph Road, on the left. In the foreground is the Delph Pond which was used as both a village curling pond and to supply water to the tannery. The tanning works was established by local shoemaker Alexander Paterson about 1806 to tan his own leather. It was taken over in 1889 by John Tullis & Son and expanded to become the largest tannery in Scotland with a weekly throughput of over 1,000 hides. Tanning continued up to the 1960s when the works was taken over for use as a plastics factory. It has since ceased production.

Glenochil Mine was intended to provide long-term industrial employment for Tullibody, but it failed. It was a controversial enough project when it was proposed by the newly established National Coal Board in 1948. The idea was to extract 3,000 tons of coal a day for 50 years from an area south of the Devon, a plan which was almost certain to cause subsidence and the flooding of 700 acres of farmland. There was a very limited public enquiry before the go-ahead was given. These mine drivers began work in

January 1952 on what was to be the largest drift mine in Britain, with two parallel mines 100 feet apart and dipping at an angle of 1 in 5 for a mile and a half. But, when the working levels were opened out, the miners discovered that an earlier generation had beaten them to it and taken out most of the coal. What was left were narrow seams and stoops – columns of coal left to support the roof which were very difficult to extract. The mine began production in December 1956, but the unequal struggle to maintain any sort of output was abandoned in June 1962. This hugely expensive investment never came close to achieving its targets and was perhaps the nationalised industry's biggest embarrassment.

After nationalisation of the coal industry in 1947 the newly established National Coal Board took stock of what it had inherited. In Scotland it found that the pits in the old heartland of Lanarkshire were worn out and there was an urgent need to develop new capacity. But there was a problem: the miners were in Lanarkshire and the expansion was planned in other mining areas where there were not enough houses. In Clackmannanshire the main development was at Glenochil, so, while the mines went down, the county council and the Scottish Special Housing Association put up new houses. Tullibody was transformed as old streets – like Main Street with its post office – were swept away to make space for what was in effect a new town.

Post Office and Street, Tullibody.

The new houses for incoming miners radically altered the layout of the old village. Trongate, seen in this early twentieth century view, was realigned to the extent that the present Main Street is closer to the line of the old Trongate than to the original Main Street. The Tron Tree in the centre of the picture was planted to commemorate Tullibody's local military hero, Sir Ralph Abercromby. He was in command of the British Army when it landed at Aboukir Bay in Egypt on 8 March 1801. A soldier's soldier, he was in the thick of the action as the troops fought a series of engagements with the French while advancing on Alexandria. In the final victorious battle for the city, on 21 March, Sir Ralph received a bullet wound to the thigh and died a week later.

WAR MEMORIAL, TULLIBODY.

Military heroes from another conflict were honoured in October 1921 when nearly 3,000 people witnessed the unveiling of the Tullibody and Cambus war memorial. The centrepiece of the small memorial park was a large boulder known as Samson's Button, with, set into it, a replica of the stone cross which commemorated Kenneth MacAlpine's victory over the Picts in AD 834. A brass plaque bearing the names of the men of the two villages who fell during the First World War was let into the stone. The memorial stones were surrounded by a pond, which in turn had wooden benches set around it creating a space for peaceful contemplation. The whole was paid for by public subscription, augmented by a generous donation from J. Kennedy Tullis of the tannery. Donations made by ex-servicemen were used specifically to pay for the lych gate (inset) that forms the entrance to the park. The names that were inscribed on the memorial were intended 'to live forever', but sadly it has fallen victim to neglect and vandalism, and the commemorative plaques have been removed. At the time of writing, the council is working to return the site to some semblance of its former dignity.

ABERCROMBIE SCHOOL, TULLIBODY.

B.9021.

In the early 1950s Tullibody's existing institutions would have been wholly inadequate to cope with the influx of so many mining families, so it was not just houses and shops that were built. This new primary school, named the Abercromby School, was built on a site adjacent to the War Memorial Gardens in 1951. It was designed by county architect W. H. Henry and included provision to cater for other community services as well as its principal educational function.

Baingle Brae, Tullibody.

The redevelopment of Tullibody in the 1950s swept away this view from the top of Baingle Brae looking towards Main Street. The building just creeping into the left-hand edge of the picture is one of the few from the old village to have survived and is now used as the Tullibody Working Men's Club. The area in front where the children are standing is now a car park. The high wall on the right, with the tree rising over it, was the perimeter wall of Baingle Brae House.

RELIABLE SERIES.

Baingle Brae House and its seven acres of beautiful gardens were, like most of old Tullibody, lost in the redevelopment of the 1950s. The house was built in 1834 for Alexander Paterson, the proprietor of the tannery, who had it designed after he had visited Italy and been inspired by the country villas he had seen there.

ARNSBRAE HOUSE, ALLOA.

Arnsbrae House, which sits screened by trees from the Alloa to Stirling road, was built in 1885 to the designs of Alfred Waterhouse, the architect responsible for Alloa Town Hall. It was later extended by Paul Waterhouse.

Alloa's original golf course at Braehead sat alongside the grounds of Arnsbrae House. It could have fallen into disuse when Alloa Golf Club moved to a new course at Schawpark in the 1930s, but some golfers, unhappy at the move, formed a new club and continued to use the course seen here at Braehead.

Tullibody House, the home of the Abercromby family, was built about 1710. It replaced an earlier building and was set beside the Forth, to the south of Braehead and to the east of Cambus. The Abercrombys had a major influence on Tullibody and on the wider world. George, son of the second laird, Alexander, was a Professor of Law at Edinburgh University, an agricultural improver and founder of the Highland Society. His eldest son, Sir Ralph, was the general who won the battle for Alexandria; another son, Sir Robert, became Governor of Bombay and one of Sir Ralph's sons, James, was Speaker of the House of Commons and became Lord Dunfermline. The house, a fine example of old Scots architecture, was eventually overtaken by the march of industrial progress and was demolished in the 1960s.

Cambus sits a short distance from the shores of the Forth, on the eastern bank of the Devon. This river of many facets starts high in the Ochils flowing east to Glendevon where it turns south-east and tumbles down to the aptly named Crook of Devon. There a dramatic bend turns it back on itself to go west, roaring down a rocky ravine at the equally well named Rumbling Bridge and cascading through the waterfalls of the Cauldron Linn. It flows swiftly into Clackmannanshire at Dollar and then twists and turns along the base of the Ochils to Menstrie where it alters course again and heads south-east to Cambus, to sweep round a last 180 degree bend before entering the Forth. The entrepreneurs who set up the Devon Ironworks thought about canalising the river from Cambus to the works at Old Sauchie, but while being an eminently practical scheme this was never carried out. A dam was, however, thrown across the Devon at Cambus, above the high tide mark, to provide a head of water to drive mills on both banks.

SAW MILL, CAMBUS.

This sawmill stood on the west bank of the Devon and is seen here looking across from the main village of Cambus. While it and other mills made use of the water coming down the river as their source of power, the main industries of the village, distilling and brewing, looked the other way to the Forth. To modern eyes the idea of Cambus being a port may seem unlikely, but it was capable of berthing small ships which brought in supplies of grain and took out the whisky and beer. Brewing was established on a commercial scale in 1792 and distilling by 1806. The brewery was moved to beside the new railway in the 1860s and continued in production until the 1950s when the site was taken over for the production of malt whisky.